THE COUPLE'S ADVENTURE GUIDE

THE COUPLE'S ADVENTURE GUIDE

CARMEN WILDE

CONTENTS

Introduction to the World of Couple's Adventures

Welcome to the world of couple's adventures! Imagine embarking on thrilling journeys that not only allow you to explore the world's beauty but also bring you and your partner closer. Whether it's scaling a mountain, wandering through ancient ruins, or simply strolling through a new city, adventures provide the perfect backdrop for deepening your bond as a couple.

Think about it: you and your best friend, hand in hand, discovering new places, cultures, and experiences. It's not just about the destination; it's about the shared moments, the laughter, the challenges, and the triumphs along the way. We hope this book ignites your imagination, fueling your excitement for planning these incredible adventures together.

Anticipating travel and adventure fosters connections from the get-go. The excitement and preparation stage is a treasure trove of bonding opportunities. Picture yourselves, curled up on the couch with maps and travel guides, dreaming up itineraries and sharing your hopes and dreams. It's a chance to understand each other in new ways, as you navigate the fun (and sometimes stressful) journey of planning.

Planning and dreaming are more than logistical tasks—they're opportunities to explore what truly matters to you both. These early stages help reveal areas of agreement and potential conflict, paving the way for complementary dreams. And don't forget to keep a record of these fun conversations! Later on, you can look back and see how your shared journey began and relive those moments of joy and love, even if you encountered a few bumps along the way.

Adventures play a significant role in your lives together. However, in our busy world, finding time for them can be challenging. The key is to approach your adventure intentions with a practical mindset. You don't have to drop everything—you can strike a balance. Contrary to popular belief, adventures and budgeting are not mutually exclusive. We believe in carving out space in the budget for what truly matters. Tracking spending habits closely can make these good intentions more realistic.

So, why are couple's adventures important? What exactly is a couple's adventure? Sure, travel is a big part of it, but it goes deeper than that. It's about recognizing that the best things in life aren't just about what you do—it's about who you become together.

Understanding the Benefits of Adventure for Couples

Welcome to "The Couple's Adventure Guide: Plan, Dream, and Celebrate Together." Creating this guide has been an adventure in itself! Let's celebrate reaching this point—it's the first step in what I hope will be an incredibly fulfilling journey for you and your partner. The project's delay due to the arrival of our first grandchild was a blessing in disguise, allowing us to gather even more valuable insights. At times, Bob and I discussed whether to continue, but I'm so glad we persevered.

Trusting in this tool and putting in the hard work to complete it will result in something you can all be proud of. Imagine this as the beginning of your first true adventure as a couple!

I firmly believe in the benefits of adventure for couples. Adventure doesn't always come easily, but the effort is well worth it. Some of our best memories were created while facing challenges together. Shared experiences allow partners to learn more about themselves and each other. I've discovered aspects of my husband I might never have known without the nudge of shared adventure adversity.

Adventures often have clear goals or achievements, offering both novices and seasoned explorers the chance to showcase their skills and abilities. This helps to level the playing field and balance the power dynamics that may exist in everyday communication styles between couples. It's a chance to see your partner in a new light and appreciate their strengths.

CHAPTER 1

Planning Your Couple's Adventure

Planning a couple's adventure is about diving into a sea of new possibilities and daring to dream big together. It's an exhilarating mix of hope and celebration, recognizing each small step you both take towards your shared goals. These little moments—whether it's exploring a new restaurant or picking out whimsical wooden puzzle pieces for a guest book—become the cherished memories that shape your adventure. Every detail adds a unique touch to your vision, be it for a wedding or any other significant journey you plan together.

In today's fast-paced world, meticulous planning is essential. While the word "planning" might conjure images of tedious tasks, it's important to remember that real-life adventures don't just happen by chance. Every exciting journey is the result of people who dare to dream, take risks, and put in the effort to make their dreams a reality.

Setting Shared Goals and Expectations

When planning an adventure together, it's natural for partners to have varying levels of enthusiasm, skepticism, and expectations. One person might be over-the-moon excited, while the other might be indifferent or even apprehensive. It's crucial to understand that both of your perspectives matter. This is where aligning your goals and expectations comes into play.

Every relationship is unique, and so are its goals. Experts recommend ensuring that both partners' expectations and plans are in harmony. This means openly discussing and acknowledging what each person hopes to gain from the adventure, both individually and as a couple. Clear communication is the cornerstone of this process.

Take time to express out loud what you're each anticipating—not just regarding the trip itself, but also during the planning stages. You might discover how differently you each handle the other person's dreams. If your partner's dream doesn't fully resonate with you, that's okay. It's an opportunity to decide if you want to find a middle ground or perhaps take a different path. Establishing the desired outcomes will help you create a unified approach.

As couples counselor Dr. Andy Hansen suggests, "When couples are on the same page—or at least within the same chapter of the book—setting your adventure goals becomes more meaningful. What does each person hope to achieve from this experience? What memories, connections, and values do you want to create together? Planning with a clear purpose provides a reference point as tension, stress, or uncertainty arises."

Remember, this is about building memories and strengthening your bond. Each adventure is a stepping stone in your shared journey, and the planning process itself is an integral part of that adventure. Embrace it with enthusiasm and openness, and you'll find that the journey becomes as rewarding as the destination.

CHAPTER 2

Choosing the Perfect Adventure Destination

One of the delightful parts of planning a couple's adventure is selecting the perfect destination. Before you dive into the specifics, it's essential to choose a location that captivates both your interests. This will be your dream vacation spot, a place where you can both unwind and create beautiful memories together.

To ensure your trip is stress-free and enjoyable, start by considering your interests and activity levels. Some couples thrive in the outdoors, enjoying camping in the wilderness, while others prefer the luxuries of a comfy hotel room, concierge services, and a bottle of fine wine before bed. It's crucial to be honest and upfront about your travel preferences to minimize differences. Discussing these options can help you both agree on what kind of experience you want:

- **Do you want to explore a place you've never been before?** Discovering new parts of the country or the world can be thrilling, but it's essential to ensure it fits your budget.
- **Private or crowded location?** Some couples enjoy the lively atmosphere of popular tourist spots, while others seek more tranquil, secluded destinations.

- **Solo or group adventure?** Decide if you want to have a private journey for just the two of you or if you'd prefer to share the experience with friends, family, or a community group.
- **Domestic or international?** Traveling abroad can be a fantastic adventure but consider any limitations, such as budgets, health concerns, and travel restrictions.
- **Types of experiences?** From cultural activities, art, and music to culinary adventures—like tasting new cuisines or taking cooking classes—there's a wide range of experiences to choose from.

Factors to Consider When Selecting a Destination

When you're choosing a destination, there are several critical factors to weigh together:

1. **What will make this trip amazing for you both?** Think about your priorities. Is safety the most crucial aspect? Or maybe it's the chance to recharge and relax. Perhaps you're after a shared experience ticking off a bucket-list destination, or maybe you're excited about engaging in various activities.
2. **Price considerations:** From activities and dining to parking, all costs should be evaluated. While budget is important, it shouldn't come at the expense of fulfilling a dream adventure, like visiting a world-famous location.
3. **Research:** For less experienced travelers, researching can help narrow down suitable destinations. Use resources like travel guides, websites, and apps (e.g., Google Earth, 10Best, AroundMe) to explore potential spots. Review photos, read reviews, and compare options to see what matches your interests.

4. **Time and financial planning:** How far in advance are you planning? Can you afford deposits and spread out expenses over several months? Realistically assess your time off from work and personal commitments. If you have health concerns or lack travel insurance, international travel might not be the best option.

Consider the following steps:

- **List potential destinations**: Based on your shared interests, create a shortlist of potential destinations.
- **Detailed research**: Look at key details like climate, high and low tourist seasons, local activities, and necessary reservations.
- **Plan ahead**: Use spreadsheets to track crucial information—weather patterns, population, altitude, and other data that could impact your vacation experience.
- **Compare and decide**: Evaluate your options, weigh the pros and cons, and make a decision that excites and suits both of you.

By taking the time to consider these factors, you'll create a solid foundation for an unforgettable adventure together. Let's make that dream trip happen step by step, with each detail ensuring a perfect and memorable journey.

CHAPTER 3

Packing Essentials for Your Couple's Adventure

Whether you're seasoned adventurers or embarking on your first romantic getaway, spending time in a spectacular setting can significantly enhance your bond. However, preparing for such an excursion requires thorough planning and commitment. Here's a guide to ensure you pack all the essentials for a smooth and enjoyable journey.

The key to a successful couple's adventure lies in preparation. Packing smartly involves thinking ahead and considering all your needs. Let's break it down:

- **Choose your bag wisely:** The type of bag you pick depends on your destination, the duration of your trip, and what you plan to bring. Think about whether you need a backpack for a hiking trip or a suitcase for a city break.
- **Prepare the four Cs:** Approach your adventure with the four Cs in mind: Comfort, Convenience, Comprehensive planning, and Connectivity. These principles will help make your travels smoother and more enjoyable.

Creating a Comprehensive Packing List

Start by deciding what to carry based on your destination and activities. Here are some steps to help you create an efficient packing list:

1. **Choose the right bag:**
   ◦ Ensure it's suitable for your destination and easy to carry.
   ◦ Consider a durable, lightweight backpack for active trips or a rolling suitcase for urban adventures.
2. **Making a list:**
   ◦ **Categories:** Divide your items into categories: clothes, personal care, tech equipment, medical supplies, documents, and miscellaneous.
   ◦ **Prioritize:** Organize your items by priority. Knowing what's essential helps avoid stress and ensures you don't forget crucial items.
3. **Clothing and gear:**
   ◦ **Weather-appropriate attire:** Pack clothes suitable for the climate and activities planned.
   ◦ **Layering:** Include layers for changing weather conditions.
   ◦ **Footwear:** Bring comfortable, versatile shoes for walking, hiking, or formal events.
   ◦ **Specialized gear:** If your trip involves specific activities like camping, skiing, or diving, pack the necessary equipment.
4. **Personal care items:**
   ◦ Travel-sized toiletries: Shampoo, conditioner, body wash, toothpaste, etc.
   ◦ Skincare essentials: Sunscreen, moisturizer, lip balm.

- First aid kit: Bandages, antiseptics, any personal medications.

5. **Tech equipment:**
   - **Chargers and batteries:** Ensure you have chargers for all your electronic devices.
   - **Power bank:** A portable battery pack can be a lifesaver, especially in remote areas.
   - **Camera/GoPro:** Capture your memories in high quality.

6. **Important documents:**
   - **Identification:** Passports, driver's licenses, travel insurance documents.
   - **Reservation details:** Hotel bookings, activity reservations, flight tickets.
   - **Backup copies:** Keep digital and physical copies of essential documents.

7. **Miscellaneous:**
   - **Travel guides:** Bring any books, maps, or apps to help navigate your destination.
   - **Reusable water bottles:** Stay hydrated without relying on single-use plastics.
   - **Snacks:** Pack some energy bars, nuts, or dried fruits for quick energy boosts.

8. **Connecting essentials:**
   - **Communication:** Ensure you have a way to stay connected, such as a mobile phone or satellite device if you're going off the grid.
   - **Travel apps:** Install helpful travel apps for navigation, translation, and discovering local spots.

By creating and adhering to a comprehensive packing list, you ensure a stress-free, enjoyable adventure. Remember, every step of preparation brings you closer to the journey of a lifetime. Happy travels!

CHAPTER 4

Outdoor Skills and Safety for Couples

Preparedness is invaluable when it comes to outdoor safety. Being ready to tackle unexpected challenges is the best way to stay safe in the great outdoors. While you don't need to train as extreme adventure experts to enjoy your time in the woods, having a basic skill set is essential. Couples who can read maps, plan and manage time, use basic outdoor tools, respond accurately to changing weather and terrain, remain calm if they get lost, and focus on problem-solving will have the confidence and skills needed for a safe, fun, and enriching experience. Once these foundational skills are mastered, you can consider other techniques and ideas, especially when hiking with a group, particularly when children or less experienced hikers are involved.

Navigating and Surviving in the Wilderness

You don't have to be born with outdoor savvy to navigate and survive in the wilderness. Success lies in continuous learning, practical application, and remaining calm under pressure. Here are some key skills and strategies to master:

1. **Map Reading and Navigation:**

- **Learn to read topographic maps:** Understand the symbols and contour lines to gauge the terrain.
- **Use a compass or GPS:** Ensure you know how to correctly use a compass and, if available, a GPS device to navigate.
- **Mark your trail:** Use physical markers or a GPS app to keep track of your path.

2. **Time Management:**
   - **Plan your itinerary:** Break down your journey into manageable segments with estimated timeframes.
   - **Set a pace:** Adjust your speed to ensure you reach safe spots (like campsites) before nightfall.

3. **Basic Outdoor Tools:**
   - **Pack essential tools:** Bring items like a multi-tool, knife, fire starter, and repair kit.
   - **First-aid kit:** Always carry a well-stocked first-aid kit, tailored to address common outdoor injuries and personal health needs.

4. **Weather Awareness:**
   - **Monitor weather forecasts:** Before and during your trip, track weather updates.
   - **React to changes:** Have a plan for sudden changes in weather and know how to build a temporary shelter if needed.

5. **Problem-Solving:**
   - **Stay calm:** In any adverse situation, remaining calm is crucial.
   - **Assess the situation:** Analyze the problem and determine the safest course of action.
   - **Act on your plan:** With confidence and clear-headedness, execute your plan.

6. **Communication:**
   - **Discuss fears and doubts:** Have open conversations about any apprehensions before and during the trip.
   - **Check-in regularly:** Communicate your location and status with each other to ensure safety.

Additional Survival Tips

1. **Trust Your Instincts:**
   - **Gut feelings:** Trusting your instincts can guide you through uncertain situations.
   - **Back it up:** Combine instinct with practical knowledge and experience to make sound decisions.
2. **Stay Informed About Hazards:**
   - **Recognize risks:** Know the potential hazards, including signs of hypothermia, dehydration, and altitude sickness.
   - **Act promptly:** Address these hazards quickly to avoid worsening conditions.
3. **Make Safe Choices:**
   - **Decisions:** Continuously make decisions that prioritize safety over risk.
   - **Injuries:** Know basic first-aid to address injuries on the trail.
   - **Disorders:** Be aware of common outdoor-related disorders and their preventive measures.

Remember, good wilderness travel is about making a series of calculated choices to reduce risk. With proper preparation, clear communication, and a focus on safety, you and your partner can enjoy a fantastic outdoor adventure.

CHAPTER 5

Capturing Memories: Photography and Journaling Tip

L ife is a journey, and our adventures deserve to be documented and preserved. A century ago, adventurers hired local artists to paint their explorations. In such amazing places with our current era, we can easily get lost in their beauty, sometimes forgetting the value of our own memories. Capturing and preserving these moments through photos and journaling provides a detailed account of our adventures—both good and bad—that we'll cherish in the future. This ultimate keepsake is one of the best ways to immortalize a lifetime of traveling.

Preserving Moments for a Lifetime

Travel experiences are fleeting, but their memories can warm your heart and lift your spirit for life. Imagine being able to bottle a piece of your adventures and relive them vividly, transcending time. This may seem daunting, as it requires perfecting various forms of expression, but it's more achievable than you think!

Photography is adaptable and accessible to everyone, requiring no specific skills. Focus on capturing the personality of a place, which can be more compelling than simply snapping parts of it.

Recording your thoughts, fears, love, and joy on paper becomes a treasure that's uniquely yours. Keeping a journal need not be intimidating. It can be whimsical, personal, and free-flowing—no one else needs to read what you write. Whether you jot down terse entries or let your thoughts ramble, the key is capturing your experiences in a way that resonates with you and your travel companion.

A sketchbook is another fantastic method to preserve your memories. Don't worry if your drawings aren't perfect; having a physical copy of your memories is what truly matters. Sketch your accommodations, bustling markets, picturesque streets, and of course, each other.

Tips for Capturing Memories

Here are some tips that have worked for us and can work for you too:

1. **Good photos are essential:** Digital memories can be lost, so it's important to take high-quality photos that matter to you personally. Invest in good equipment and seek advice from photo enthusiasts.
2. **Use both regular and digital cameras:** While digital shots offer immediacy and convenience without the need for photo labs, film photography provides clarity and detail. We also love Polaroids for their nostalgic charm.
3. **Capture the personality of a place:** Focus on what makes a location unique—its ambiance, people, and culture. These photos will evoke more emotion and memories than generic landscapes.
4. **Journaling:** Don't be intimidated by the idea of keeping a journal. Write freely and let your thoughts flow. Document your emotions, experiences, and reflections.

5. **Create a sketchbook:** Sketching can be a wonderful way to capture memories. Your drawings don't have to be perfect—what matters is preserving your adventures in a tactile format.

Remember, every photo taken and word written is a way to hold onto a piece of your journey forever. These keepsakes will help you revisit your travels long after you've returned home.

CHAPTER 6

Budgeting and Financial Planning for Couple's Adve

B udgeting and financial planning are crucial aspects of making your couple's adventures a reality. Did you know that experiences tend to leave lasting impressions, rather than material possessions? Research from 2014 found that purchasing experiences brings richer memories over time. While you may not be dealing with budget constraints, many people do face limits on expendable income. Discussing your budget from the onset and prioritizing your travel goals are great steps towards having those fulfilling experiences together. Remember, budgeting isn't just about the numbers—it requires the right mindset too.

One effective method is the 50/20/30 rule, which you may already be familiar with. This rule suggests allocating 50% of your income to needs, 20% to savings, and 30% to wants. By tracking both joint and individual spending over a few weeks or months, you can create a flexible adventure fund. Knowing where your money is going will help you decide which spending categories to adjust. This knowledge empowers you to save for planned adventures or spontaneous getaways. Use your shared travel priority to fuel the motivation for monitoring your spending. Determine how much you need to save each month and how much should remain in your checking account, beyond your emergency fund, for monthly expenses. Sometimes, this means redirecting your savings currently earmarked for other expenses, but with careful planning, you can achieve your adventure goals without compromising your financial stability.

Maximizing Adventure on a Budget

As adventurous souls on a budget, we've found numerous ways to cut travel costs while still covering our everyday living expenses. Here are some tips to make traveling more accessible and at the heart of enjoying couple's adventures:

1. **Prioritize Your Adventures:**
   ◦ Determine what matters most in your budget. When you prioritize adventures, it becomes easier to cut non-essential expenses like sodas, cable subscriptions, and dining out. Services like Mint.com can help you visualize your spending on entertainment and make adjustments.
2. **Look For Travel Deals:**
   ◦ Sign up for credit cards from airlines and train services like Southwest, Delta, Alaska, and Amtrak, which often offer sign-up bonuses in the form of flight miles or travel credits. Redeem these for future trips. Check websites like Living Social, Groupon, and Amazon Local for substantial discounts on adventure activities, vacations, and weekend getaways.
3. **Plan Dinner Dates:**
   ◦ By planning and budgeting for dinner dates at home, you can save on groceries, enjoy the cooking experience together, and stay within budget. Turn cooking into a

fun activity by having contests or experimenting with budget-friendly recipes. If dining out isn't feasible, create spontaneous date nights at home using pantry staples or engaging in fun activities like friendly cooking challenges.

4. **Resource Management with Task Pairing:**
   ○ Make everyday tasks romantic and fun to save money and enhance your bond. Turn chores like gardening, DIY projects, or meal prepping into enjoyable activities that bring you closer while also cutting costs.

By embracing these strategies, you'll find that balancing finances and adventures enriches your lives without breaking the bank. Planning together and being resourceful can lead to wonderful, affordable experiences that you'll cherish forever.

CHAPTER 7

Balancing Adventure with Relaxation and Romance

Balancing adventure with relaxation and romance during your couple's escapades is crucial for a memorable and fulfilling experience. Adventures bring excitement and thrill, while relaxation and romance provide moments of connection and rejuvenation. The way you weave these elements together will define how your memories and experiences unfold after your adventure.

Integrating relaxation into your adventures can be as simple as choosing activities that require less exertion, allowing you to enjoy the moment without feeling overwhelmed. Romantic experiences are also essential for couples, adding a layer of intimacy and joy to your journey. Whether it's a spontaneous picnic in a secluded spot or a candlelit dinner under the stars, these moments of romance enhance the overall experience.

Creating Intimate Moments in Nature

What better backdrop than nature to kindle the warmth of connection and create lifelong memories? Here are some approaches and suggestions to foster intimacy and romantic connections in the great outdoors:

1. **Plan Together:**
   - Involve your partner in planning the expedition. Discuss your preferences, interests, and expectations. Collaborative planning ensures that both of you have a say in the adventure and creates a sense of shared responsibility and excitement.

2. **Keep a Shared Journal:**
   - Encourage personal diary-keeping or maintain a shared journal where both of you can document your thoughts, experiences, and reflections. This practice helps you capture the essence of your journey and provides a treasure trove of memories to look back on.

3. **Create Poetic Memories:**
   - Embrace the poet and muse dynamic by writing poems or creating stories together. Try a "team shout-poem" with alternating lines or a "pass-the-paper" group poem. These creative activities foster deep connections and bring out the romantic in both of you.

4. **Engage in Heartfelt Conversations:**
   - Use the serene environment to have open and honest conversations about your hopes, dreams, and relationship. Discussing your aspirations and sharing your feelings can strengthen your bond and create cherished memories.

5. **Enjoy Simple Luxuries:**
   - Plan for moments of relaxation amidst your adventures. Consider indulging in a massage, soaking in a hot tub, or sharing a bottle of fine wine while watching the sunset. These simple luxuries provide a perfect balance to adventurous activities and allow you to unwind and connect.

6. **Spontaneous Romantic Gestures:**
    ◦ Make a habit of creating spontaneous romantic moments. Whether it's surprising your partner with breakfast in bed, a handwritten love note, or a thoughtful gesture, these acts of love create lasting impressions.

Remember, the aim is to create a harmonious blend of adventure, relaxation, and romance. After a thrilling adventure, take time to relax and do nothing in an interesting, romantic location. Perhaps a dreamy secluded getaway in Montana or a cozy mountain cabin can provide the perfect setting for post-adventure relaxation and romance. Embrace these moments to unwind, reflect on your journey, and enjoy the company of each other.

By deliberately fostering these intimate moments, you not only enhance your adventure but also create a rich tapestry of memories that will be cherished for years to come.

CHAPTER 8

Celebrating Milestones and Achievements Together

There's something magical about marking a special moment with your partner. Not only does it acknowledge the significance of that moment, but it also solidifies your shared success. Celebrating a round-number anniversary, a major achievement, or a personal success can create lasting memories.

For instance, imagine celebrating your six-month anniversary on the exact day it occurs. It's a wonderful way to honor your journey together and perhaps add a bit of elegant bubbly, a small gift, or a local toast to your celebration.

Additionally, consider making one day of every week your 'big' day during your trip. This approach ensures you have something to look forward to and celebrate regularly. These small, consistent joys become integral to your overall adventure, pushing boundaries and fulfilling dreams.

Reflect back on the dreams you listed at the beginning of your journey. Celebrate every milestone, whether reaching a significant goal or making an agreement to pursue a dream soon. Commemorate these special moments in ways that resonate with both of you.

Reflecting on Growth and Accomplishments

Learning from and appreciating our adventures and the growth they inspire is essential. As individuals and partners, we constantly evolve, face new challenges, and learn. Reflecting on growth and accomplishments is a journey of introspection and mutual recognition. It's a chance to say, "Wow, look at how far we've come," to each other.

Our adventure journeys often resemble climbing a mountain. The satisfaction of reaching the summit lies in the breathtaking journey it took to get there. Reflect on the ripple effects our adventures have on our future selves and relationships. How have these experiences allowed us to reach new heights in our personal, professional, and spiritual lives?

Hidden pearls of wisdom are scattered throughout our journeys. Seek these pearls, as they offer deeper insights into ourselves, our relationships, and the world around us. Celebrate not just the big moments of rapid change but also the slow, constant threads of personal growth.

In times of feeling stuck or overwhelmed, look back on your strength, perseverance, and collective wisdom. Toast to your journey and the adventures that have brought you to this point. Recognize that every step forward, every challenge overcome, and every joy shared brings you closer to new heights and new adventures.

CHAPTER 9

Maintaining Communication and Resolving Conflicts

To maintain a healthy relationship during your journey, effective communication is key. It's essential to express your needs before, during, and after the adventure. While you might share many dreams, it's important to recognize that not all dreams will be shared. Listening to each other's goals and aspirations is crucial for mutual understanding and support.

Travels and adventures often take couples out of their usual, well-controlled environments and place them in unpredictable situations. This can sometimes lead to conflicts about plans, activities, finances, and responsibilities. Effective communication helps couples successfully navigate these challenges and stay connected.

Conflicts are a natural part of any close relationship. It's common for arguments to arise more frequently during trips due to the added stress and unfamiliarity. However, these conflicts don't have to derail your adventure. Remember, you're dynamic problem-solvers. When conflicts arise, approach them calmly and constructively. Here are some strategies to help maintain effective communication and resolve conflicts during your adventures:

Effective Communication Strategies for Couples

1. **The No-Surprises Rule:**
   - Adventures are full of unknowns, but surprises that could have been anticipated are less appealing. Communicate openly about your expectations, preferences, and concerns in advance. This reduces misunderstandings and sets the stage for a smoother journey.
2. **Active Listening:**
   - Take the time to listen to your partner's thoughts and feelings without interrupting. Acknowledge their perspective and show empathy. This creates a supportive environment where both partners feel heard and valued.
3. **Share Decision-Making:**
   - Involve each other in the decision-making process. Share responsibilities and make joint decisions about itinerary, activities, and expenses. This ensures that both partners have a say and reduces the likelihood of conflicts.
4. **Stay Flexible:**
   - Be prepared to adapt and compromise. Traveling can be unpredictable, and plans may need to change. Flexibility allows you to navigate unexpected situations with grace and maintain a positive attitude.
5. **Express Your Needs:**
   - Don't be afraid to voice your needs and preferences. Whether it's needing downtime, seeking adventure, or wanting to try new experiences, clearly express what you need to feel comfortable and happy.
6. **Conflict Resolution Techniques:**

○ When conflicts arise, focus on problem-solving rather than placing blame. Use "I" statements to express your feelings and needs without accusing your partner. For example, say "I feel frustrated when..." instead of "You always..."

7. **Regular Check-Ins:**
   ○ Schedule regular check-ins to discuss how you're both feeling and address any concerns. These check-ins provide an opportunity to reconnect and ensure that both partners are on the same page.

8. **Plan Romantic and Relaxing Moments:**
   ○ Balance your adventures with moments of relaxation and romance. Plan activities that allow you to unwind and connect on a deeper level. Whether it's a quiet dinner, a walk on the beach, or a hot tub session, these moments help strengthen your bond.

By incorporating these communication strategies, you'll create a supportive and harmonious environment that enhances your adventure. Remember, effective communication isn't about eliminating all surprises or conflicts but about navigating them together with understanding and empathy. Your shared journey will be richer and more fulfilling when both partners feel heard, valued, and connected.

CHAPTER 10

Sustaining the Adventure Spirit in Everyday Life

The force of adventure isn't confined to grand journeys or weekend getaways. It can gradually become a part of your personality, philosophy, and the very soul of your everyday life. Planning, dreaming, and celebrating this adventurous spirit with your loved one can bring purpose and joy to even the most mundane tasks. When two hearts, enriched with practical wisdom, aim for the same goal, it's more than just a game—it's a fulfilling reality.

Keeping that adventure spirit alive is crucial, even during the routine periods of life when camping and privacy seem out of reach. Many of us agree that occasional wilderness wanderings are beneficial: they heal the spirit, refresh the mind, and strengthen our love. But there's no reason why a similar undercurrent of adventure can't be maintained at home, even without money to save or vacations to look forward to.

While mountain lakes, star-sprinkled skies, and majestic ranges are undeniably captivating, we must also learn to find joy and adventure in the everyday moments. The sharp spice of life's journey may seem absent when yearning for distant thunderstorms, but we can savor the small excitements of our daily routine. Avoid valuing only the grand adventures and learn to appreciate the beauty in everyday life.

Possibly adjusting:

Interacting with Others Who Share a Love for Adventure
Engaging with friends or communities who share your enthusiasm for adventure can breed excitement about life's little pleasures. Have you enjoyed a particularly lovely day exploring the city? Share that highlight with a friend and cherish that moment together. As time passes, keep reminding each other to focus on fun and create new memories together. Sharing these highlights can help couples maintain an ongoing "honeymoon" lifestyle.

Incorporating Adventure into Daily Routines
Adventure lies in the perspective, not the extravagance. Here are some practical ways to infuse daily life with an adventurous spirit:

1. **Make Day Trips a Habit:**
   - Plan regular day trips to explore nearby towns, parks, or hidden gems. Discovering new places doesn't always require long travels or extended vacations.
2. **Find Adventure in Everyday Tasks:**
   - Turn routine activities into mini-adventures. Challenge yourselves to try new recipes, explore different neighborhoods, or experiment with gardening or DIY projects.
3. **Bring Vacation Vibes Home:**
   - Relive your favorite travel experiences by incorporating elements of those trips into your daily life. Cook dishes you discovered abroad, play music that reminds you of your travels, or decorate your home with souvenirs and mementos.
4. **Embrace the Thrill of the Hunt:**

- Explore antique stores, thrift shops, or flea markets for unique finds. The excitement of discovering hidden treasures can bring a sense of adventure to your everyday life.

5. **Create Spontaneous Fun:**
   - Plan spontaneous date nights or surprise activities. Whether it's a last-minute picnic in the park, a movie marathon, or a cozy indoor campout, these activities can add a spark to your routine.

6. **Connect with Nature:**
   - Spend time outdoors, even if it's in your own backyard. Go for walks, have a barbecue, or simply sit and enjoy the fresh air. Nature has a way of bringing tranquility and adventure into our lives.

By incorporating these simple yet meaningful activities into your daily routines, you can sustain the adventure spirit and continue to create special memories with your partner. Adventure doesn't always have to be grand—it can be found in the small, everyday moments that make life exciting and fulfilling.

Conclusion: Embracing the Journey Together

The most profound insight this guide offers is this: The single most momentous adventure you will embark on as a couple is the one in which you both commit to embracing adventures together. Through every twist and turn in your journey through life, it's the solidarity of facing the unknown together that will put you among the most connected, fulfilled couples you'll ever meet.

Embrace the adventure of planning your journeys together. Dream big, reflect deeply, and take intentional steps today to create the life you want together. Celebrating an adventure together symbolically reenacts your shared journey. Your collective memories make a statement about who you are and, more importantly, who you are to each other. They demonstrate your values, how you spend your precious time, and the people and experiences that matter most to you. In essence, they powerfully reflect what you, as a couple, find wonderful and meaningful.

The majesty lies in this precious and unique combination of people, time, and experiences. Out of the 1.3 billion bits of information swirling around you at any moment, there's a special someone that makes your moment significant. That shared space is packed with your wisdom, accomplishments, and shared laughter.

This is the slow, beautifully smeared whirl of adventure. This is you, me, and all the **us** moments splashed throughout time. As we are now, the adventure continues.